Advent Worship Companion:

Lectionary Year C

By

Carole R. Fontaine

Fontaine, Carole R.

Advent Worship Companion: Lectionary Year C

Publishing and printed by LuLu.com in the United States of America

ISBN 978-0-557-12669-9

A product of:

Greenheart Studio

and

Fontaine Associates

Table of Contents

Acknowledgements

Images provided with our videos come from a variety of sources: original art by the author, based on ancient Near Eastern artifacts, photographs taken in a variety of archaeological collections by the author and her mate, Dr. Craig Fontaine, and some by Jennifer Shaw, Faculty Assistant at Andover Newton Theological School. We would also like to thank here the good people of Sacred Destinations (www.sacred-destinations.com) for their permissions to use their extensive collection of geographical and artistic images of the Biblical World and Christianity. We commend them to you, as a fine site that makes images available for all sorts of religious and congregational purposes, copyright free and without cost to the Church. We are exceedingly grateful to them for their work, and its availability.

Any such enterprise as this one requires a lot of help 'behind the scenes/texts/cameras', so we would like to express our thanks to Lay Choir Director Jennifer Shaw for her invaluable suggestions on music and assistance in filming. We would also like to thank Robert Craigue of the Massachusetts Bible Society Media Center on the campus of Andover Newton Theological School for his work on camera, editing and conceptualization. Craig Fontaine, as always, lent his expertise to this production in a variety of ways, and was responsible for the formatting and editing of this document.

Finally, some of the work produced here was made possible by a sabbatical leave granted by Andover Newton Theological School, and funded by the Henry Luce III Foundation Fellowships in Theology (2008-09), as well as generous donations from the congregation of Pass-a-Grille Beach Community Church. We would also like to thank the National Office of the United Church of Christ for their support of our video ministries.

Preface

Welcome, and thank you for your consideration and support of this ministry. We hope that the materials presented here, both in video and written form, will assist in making Advent a meaningful experience.

Our goal for this project is to strengthen pastors and their congregations by providing good, progressive Biblical scholarship, grounded in the most recent Biblical research, in the most cost effective and direct manner available. It has been apparent to us that such resources are not necessarily easily accessible or affordable for many congregations, especially those located in less urban or affluent areas. Likewise, attending a conference where world class scholars are present is often cost prohibitive for many clergy. This is our effort to "bridge" that gap between professor/theologian and parish by offering a resource that we hope can be used to support preaching, assist with worship, and aid in adult study.

This material is presented in two parts:

- ❖ First, there is a four-week video presentation by Dr. Carole Fontaine that can be viewed and/or downloaded for use by clergy for preaching or worship. This can also be used as a part of an adult Advent Bible study. Because this material follows the lectionary, there is a real opportunity to tie education and worship together during this season.

- ❖ Second, there is a written, downloadable Companion guide that provides, not only exegesis, but also ideas for worship and music (including prayers and quotes), as well as "starter" ideas for adult study and discussion. We recognize that some of the musical selections (contemporary) are not sensitive to inclusive language, but we leave the use of this genre, and its appropriateness, to discretion of your congregation.

We welcome your thoughts and suggestions as this project continues to evolve, and its success is ultimately measured by its value for you. This material is our offering to you. If you find it beneficial and would like to support us in this endeavor, we would welcome your offering in return. A $10.00 donation would be most appreciated for viewing/downloading the group of our video offerings. This Companion guide is available for download or as published hard copy at a modest cost to cover production. The Pay Pal links provided are both an easy and secure means for doing this.

Thanks for your participation in this Advent effort. We pray that the upcoming season will be both joyful and fruitful for you, and your congregation. Blessings and peace!

Rev. Keith A. Haemmelmann, D. Min.
Sr. Minister, Pass-a-Grille Beach (FL) United Church of Christ

Advent Year C:

Guide for Pastors, Bible Study Leaders and Others

Carole R. Fontaine, Ph.D.

Taylor Professor of Biblical Theology and History

Theologian in Residence, Pass-a-Grille Beach Community Church, St. Pete Beach, FL

Henry Luce III Fellow in Theology 2008-09

Introduction

This year's Advent texts usher in a season of readings that call to mind the many ways God makes known the message of salvation for all. You will see a continuous interplay between two major cultural events, the Babylonian Exile (and Return) of Hebrew Bible (=Old Testament) times, and the Occupation of the Holy Land by Rome in the time of Jesus. Our Biblical authors form their ideas of woe and wonder by reflecting on the repetition of God's similar saving acts for the people in two similar times of ethnic and cultural challenges. The videos you are watching on exegesis of the passages for each Sunday will make use of the following ongoing themes, and you are invited to make what use of them you will, since they will be recurring in the readings:

The Message or the Messenger?

Radical Reversals: All in God's Own Good Time

The Covenant 'In Which You Delight'

Shame Games and Guilt Quilts: How do we let go?

Day of the Lord, Day of Redemption?

From Exile to Homecoming: How about it?

Each Advent Sunday section contains the following materials:

- Themes for the day's lectionary readings
- Key Theological Concepts
- Potential Sermon Topics
- Memorable Quotes from the Theological Library
- Pastoral Prayer for Sunday worship
- Suggestions for Bible Study
- Suggestions for Church Decorations
- Suggestions for Hymn Selections

You will see as you read on the themes we outline introduction to each Sunday are carried through the entire congregation, and urge participation in a variety of ways: Bible Study, decorations that highlight the theology of the texts, and are all bound together in each pastoral prayer. We have also provided a few ideas for hymn selections—always understanding, of course, that each congregation has its own traditions of beloved music for this season of the church year, which must be honored as well. We are offering suggestions, not pronouncing policy, in hopes of making your task as minister/educator/ worship leader or committed layperson a bit simpler by having an 'on-call' biblical theologian provide some ideas that may inspire you and challenge your congregation.

From all of us at Pass-a-Grille Beach Community Church, we send you best wishes for a blessed Advent Season.

Carole R. Fontaine, Theologian in Residence

Rev. Keith Haemmelmann, Pastor and Director of the Video Academy

Advent Year C:

Sunday One

Guide for Pastors, Bible Study Leaders and Others

Sunday One: Signs of the Times; Messages and Messengers: Are We Listening?

Readings:

Jer 33:14-16

Psalm 25:1-10

I Thess 3:9-13

Luke 21:25-36

Key Theological Concepts:

'Promise': covenant to David from 2 Sam 7; this covenant has a forerunner in the Covenant with Abraham in Gen 12 and throughout the ancestor stories

'Righteousness': a specific duty and sign of the redeemed community

'Mercy': 'Rachamim', the love shown by a mother for her unborn child is the image for God's passionate love of the community

'Steadfast Love': 'Chesed'—like agape but with more legal overtones, since it is guaranteed by the covenant as one of things God must do to honor the divine side of the agreement

'Heavy heart': harks back to the ancient idea from Egypt that the heart is the seat of the intellect, and its deeds are weighed against justice in the afterlife. This appears also in the Book of Proverbs.

'Signs of the Times': the natural world repeatedly shares in announcing the promise and suffering because of human sin. Our signs here are: Branch of

David, heavenly bodies, the oceans and seas, global national distress, clouds, fig trees and all trees. These signs are understood as an announcement of the Apocalypse (see 'eschatology' below).

'Eschatology': from the Greek term for 'last things', the traditions about the end of the suffering of the Earth and the People; in Q source, it takes two forms: apocalyptic eschatology (the latest view, which presumes God's devastating action) and sapiential eschatology (the earlier 'wisdom' view that emphasizes human action).

Potential Sermon Topics

There are a plethora of wonderful passages and themes here from which to choose. The nervous expectations of the waiting community (don't be caught unawares, don't forget to continue to live in righteousness—all the good commandments are still in place for Christians) make a good starting place for welcoming in the Season of Advent. We will see that our Advent texts throughout the season present us with a mixture of two of the earliest strata of the Jesus traditions: the Q Source (the oral 'sayings' gospel available to Matthew and Luke) has an early layer which emphasized the nearness of the Reign of God and the absolute call to do justice for the poor, to which is later added another level of meaning, that of the Messianic Signs that point to the Apocalypse. Both these layers are absorbed into the canonical Gospels of Matthew and Luke and form the basis of the later reflections of the early church as it tries to come to terms with the death of Jesus. In this Q source, we come to the difficult conclusion that for the earliest Jesus-movement, no special significance is attached to the death of Jesus as some sort of trigger for the Apocalypse. The modern message to us from this complex formation of the written New Testament Gospels from oral and antique written sources is that we do NOT always understand the significance of history or divine acts at the time they take place; the believing community has always 'updated' its theology in relation to their own needs, experiences, and cultures. We are not being unfaithful when we press our own understanding of the Gospel into our very different, everyday lives!

What *is* the Message the Signs of the Times are trying to give us? The biblical writers pitched their views in terms of well-known theological concepts, like the Davidic covenant (Branch from David's line) which can never be invalidated, even though the people might sin and need correction. The Chesed and Rachamim that are shown the people derive from this covenant, and in joy and hope, the people are to wait and watch for their deliverance through God's fulfillment of these biblical promises.

Perhaps most interesting given the world of environmental degradation in which we live, the Bible speaks of the state of the natural world as both a source of announcements of joy and redemption (the fig tree, the Branch) AND a potent voice, through natural disasters, that something is Very Wrong. Nature imagery continues a connection to the lost 'Tree Goddess' of ancient Canaan, whose 'branch' is shown as a sign of Her blessings on all living creatures, a sort of "Madonna of Nature'. Nature also presents this imagery in conjunction to current environmental problems—land erosion, drought, wild fires, polluted ocean which threaten the food chain, famines, wars over resources, disturbances in the atmosphere. Hence, correlating the Bible's 'then' with our 'now' is a natural step the Bible means for us to take in looking over our own historical and cultural setting.

This Sunday offers a fine opportunity to link environmental and the human rights issues they raise to the coming of the Messiah, and God's plan for a just and sustainable Earth under a new Heaven. The message may not be 'apocalyptic' in its outcome (total destruction of the whole planet in the 'Second Coming'), but its certainly presents us with the images of a time when, literally, all hell is breaking loose. Believers are warned to continue to do good, wait and watch, and be ready to care for themselves and families on the day of reckoning. Nature mirrors human society's chaos, and so it is now, as we struggle to make changes before we reach the CO_2 tipping point, beyond which we will have far less success in reversing global warming and mass species die-offs. Believers will need strength to face what lies ahead, but God has promised: we will not end in floods, so we MUST move forward confidently in dealing with our global climate issues.

Memorable Quotes from our Theological Library:

J. Dominic Crossan, *Who Killed Jesus? Exposing the Roots of Anti-Semitism in the Gospel Story of The Death of Jesus*

(In discussion of the two layers of the earliest sources, first in Q, then absorbed into Matthew and Luke, the 'wisdom' or 'sayings' level (the earliest) and the later Messianic Signs level. The former view thinks everyone will see God's action and be able to live into it; the latter claims that only special 'in-groups' will know what is going on, and live through it in some way. The former was Jesus' eventual message; the latter is what an ethnocentric church WANTED the message to be!)

> 'When a people is exploited by colonial occupation, one obvious response is armed revolt or military rebellion. But sometimes that situation of oppression is experienced as so fundamentally evil and so humanly hopeless that only transcendental intervention is deemed of any use. God, and God alone, must act to restore a ruined world to justice and holiness. This demands a vision and a program that is radical, countercultural, utopian, world-negating, or, as scholars say, *eschatological*.' (p. 46)

(On 'sapiential eschatology' (wisdom)):

> 'The word *sapientia* is Latin for 'wisdom', and sapiential eschatology announces that God has given *all human beings* the wisdom to discern how, here and now in this world, one can so live that God's power, rule and dominion are evidently present to all observers. It involves a way of life now rather than a hope for life for the future….In apocalyptic eschatology, we are waiting for God to act. In sapiential eschatology, God is waiting for us to act.' (p. 47)

Pastoral Prayer for Sunday One

Holy One of Ancient Names,
From the time we first told stories to our young,
Your many names have we spoken;
Your saving deeds have we rehearsed;
Your promises we have counted upon
As we face the Signs of the Times!

Around us, the Earth trembles
And all the waters melt and roar—
Yet we know: You are not in the Earthquake;
You are not in the Storm!

Yet ever You have spoken to us
From the midst of the Whirlwind,
When we know not where to turn.

Lord, our planet suffers;
Our cultures decay,
And everyone does what seems right
In their own eyes;
We are none of us innocent;
We are none of us pure.
Our minds are on our futures,
While we ignore our current plights.

We wait for Promises left unfulfilled,
Though we have seen much fulfilled until now.
We wait, not knowing entirely what may come,
But we hope for Your strength
That we may stand firm instead of run.

Bring us into this Advent Season
With the hope of the Coming of the Messiah,
With the conviction to repent of cynicism
And our narrow concepts of Good.
Let the Sun, the Moon, the Stars,
And all that dwell beneath them,
Rejoice in Your great Gift to us!
Make our season of giving
A Season of Justice,
A time of chesed and mercy,
A light to the nations,
And a balm to the weary heart.

And let the people say,

"Amen!"

Suggestions for Bible Study of Advent C Sunday One

This Sunday's texts present an excellent opportunity to review some basic concepts from the Hebrew Bible (OT) that become so important in the message of the coming of the Messiah, and in Jesus' teachings. Using the key theological concepts, you might provide a brief history of the idea, including its most important parallel texts:

Covenant: with Noah (Gen 8:20-9:17), with Abraham (Gen 12:1-3), with Moses (Exod 6:2-8; 19:1-9), with David (2 Sam 7:1-17)

The Northern Kingdom (Israel) emphasized the 'Conditional Covenant' of Moses, which could be broken, like a treaty or contract, if either side failed to live up to their responsibilities. The Southern Kingdom of Judah used the later Davidic covenant that could NEVER be broken, and this was picked up by the New Testament writers to speak of God's eternal compassion for humanity in the redemptive work of Jesus the Christ. Both covenants had earlier antecedents in treaties and grants commonly used in the ancient Near East (i.e., 'secular' or legal concepts work perfectly well as metaphors for our many relationships with God). The Mosaic covenant looks forward to what the people MUST do; the Davidic covenant looks backward at what the faithful servant has already done.

Study questions:

1. Are there any modern 'agreements', 'treaties' or 'covenants' of which we are a part? Are our duties within them considered 'sacred'? What do we do when a covenant is broken (this can cover everything from cheating in a marriage, disappointing a child over a promise made, violations of the Geneva Conventions, empty campaign promises, or promises, real or implied, between employers and employees). What promise does OUR congregation make to its members? To its Pastor and other leaders? To the Community? How do we choose to hold one another accountable?

2. What are the 'signs' of *our* times? Which concern you most? Which are under your control? Which are not? (Examples: global epidemics are a

'sign' of the interconnectedness of societies made possible by modern travel; the rise of racism in the United States since the Obama election is a 'sign' of deep discomfort in our society, which some magnify and spread for manipulative purposes of all sorts, the rise of the developing world's desire for fuel and a modern life-style contain plenty of 'signs' that tell the story of both our past (colonial exploitation of resource-rich countries) and our future (global degradation from increased use of carbon-based fuels). The point here is to focus on the Message, rather than the messengers (all the terrible happenings on earth): things are bad, getting worse, but God wills redemption and fulfillment of previous covenants. The Message is that the Messiah WILL come to you if you allow it, but it may mean changes in life-style, thoughts, and actions.

3. We are commanded to wait and watch, live in goodness and hopefulness, all the while surrounded by disturbing events that portend even worse futures. How do Christians manage this? What are the daily spiritual practices that undergird this ability to thrive and progress in an uncertain climate? How does one stay 'alert' without becoming nervous, faint-hearted, cynical or burnt out? What Scripture passages comfort you in such times? (Hint: Luke 21:32; reflect on this, and teach it as a prayer mantra to the class.) Is there any point in worrying about what is out of your control, or do the times demand a change from us, a re-engagement with the cynical ideas that we have no control, so are exempt from the struggle to respond to life with compassion and integrity.

4. David hoped to build God a 'temple' but God fulfilled this promise with a 'house' not of mortar, but of mortals in the form of the Davidic lineage that is applied later to Jesus. Again and again, the people expect material glories, when God seems to be much more interested in the Glorified Living (just, sustainable, transforming communities)! What does this say about God doing and fulfilling our work through those that follow? Hence, what are WE doing today to enhance, inspire, and engender Christian hope?

Suggestions for Church Decorations

Everyone has their favorite Christmas decorations, of course, but this certainly does not exhaust the ways in which a congregation can welcome in Advent. Along with wreathes, candles and carols, we suggest that you engage your various study groups and Sunday School groups in working together to create decorations for the season.

Clearly, since our readings emphasize Nature as a Messenger of the changing times, this makes a good focus, especially for smaller children. On butcher paper, or on simple white all-purpose drawing paper rolls (ask your local suppliers for cast offs or free donations, or at least a discount—Church Schools, as we all know, are definitely NOT for Profit!), using poster paints, produce a rainbow, hangings which feature the sun, moon, and stars; a hanging of clouds (perhaps the clouds might say 'Hold on! I'm comin'!', after the famous 60s song by Sam & Dave), and flowering trees (esp. the fig) and the Branch of David. The image of the happy or weighed down heart, sitting on a scale, being balanced by Bible verses would also work with this set of readings. One could also feature the words in Hebrew/English for Chesed and Rahamim, and show them emerging in a stream from a picture of an open Bible. Have the youth present these paintings/drawings as their offerings during the regular offertory, and then hang them for the remainder of the season (simple paper hangings should do fine with removable putty to hold hook).

Purple and Blue are the Seasonal Advent colors (purple for the royal aspect of Christ the King; blue as the 'spiritual' color associated by Jews with spiritual enlightenment). Using these colors, you may also want to include traditional secular colors of red and green. In a religious context, even these colors speak of God's love at this special season. Green highlights the Bible's emphasis on Nature as one of the messengers of the Messiah. The red blooms of holly and other seasonal berries against the evergreen branches are a sign of God's covenant with the natural world and us: even in the dead of winter, we see blossoms that remind us of God's eternal provision in the fullness of the earth's produce. . If you have available evergreen branches, or holly, place them around the altar or podium.

Suggestions for Weekly Hymn Selections

SUNDAY ONE

Pilgrim Hymnal

#14 The God of Abraham Praise

#103 Come Thou Long Expected Jesus

#105 Hail to the Lord's Anointed

#444 O Day of God Draw Nigh

New Century Hymnal

#104 We Hail You God's Anointed

#112 Keep Awake, Be Always Ready

#122 Come, O Long-expected Jesus

#609 Now is the Time Approaching

Methodist Hymnal

#196 Come, Thou Long Expected Jesus

#203 Hail to the Lord's Anointed

Contemporary Hymns

Danny Daniels, You Are the Vine

Petra, Ancient of Days

Jonathan Stockstill, Let the Church Rise

Advent Year C:

Sunday Two

Guide for Pastors, Bible Study Leaders and Others

Introduction

Advent Themes for Year C

The Message or the Messenger?

The Covenant 'In Which You Delight'

Radical Reversals: All in God's Own Good Time

Shame Games and Guilt Quilts: How do we let go?

Day of the Lord, Day of Redemption?

From Exile to Homecoming: How about it?

Sunday Two: Messages, Covenants, and the Origins of Shame

Readings:

Mal 3:1-4

Baruch 5:1-9

Psalm = Luke 1:68-79

Phil 1:3-11

Luke 3:1-6

Key Theological Concepts:

Messenger ('malach-i' = 'my messenger' in Hebrew): Like every ancient King, God communicates with groups using a messenger sent to deliver the Lord's words. This is the most basic understanding of prophecy and 'prophesying'—delivering the message as one heard it, regardless of the personal consequences.

Purification: the prophet chooses the metaphor of a metallurgist to suggest how God will cleanse and renew the people: the refining process is not simply painful (it would be to humans, but we presume metal has no feelings or sensations), but plays an important part in moving into the next phase of being. After metal has been refined, it is covered with a white ash, which must be vigorously brushed away, then the product is shined to a high finish or left 'matte'. Note that once again, human activity serves as a fitting vehicle for talking about God's interactions with the community and the soul.

City as Mother: In the ancient Near East, all cities were gendered as female, because they had walls behind which they enclosed their citizens—like a womb encloses the unborn child. Similarly, the female metaphor meant that when cities were conquered, images of sexual violence against women were considered appropriate to describe the situation. Often, the 'Mother-City' in the Hebrew Bible and New Testament is thought to have become a 'prostitute' who cheated on God the Husband, and is then punished by national rape in war. Elsewhere in the ancient world, it was simply thought that the mother-city-goddess had fled from her city for various reasons, causing it to be conquered by others. Here and elsewhere, the cities of Judah grieve over their lost exiles, and seek to gather them home to the city for a family reunion characterized by greater knowledge of God's will, and rejoicing.

The Covenant in Which You Delight: again we continue to see the import of the Hebrew Bible's understanding of its covenant with God and the ancestors, renewed for the dynasty of David. While the New Testament does not always think highly of 'the Law' or the covenants in the HB, in fact both Judaism and Christianity repeatedly return to the joy, happiness and ease of knowing precisely how God would have the community behave. It is a pleasure to obey the Law (ie., 'fulfilling a mitsvah') because it brings one closer to God, and casts out fear of punishment. Redemption from enemies is also a divine duty in the covenant, and the poets look forward to that very real and material time of deliverance.

The Natural World: as in Sunday One, we see again that the natural world can both provide models for talking about God's action, but also participate in fulfilling the covenant: trees provide shade for the people, hills will make themselves low and valleys will lift themselves up when the covenant people return home from Exile. A harvest of righteousness is produced from the 'Good Tree' that automatically bears good fruit.

Potential Sermon Topics

Depending on what you included in your sermon on the first Sunday, you have a chance to take up the particular themes that are repeated in this Sunday's texts:

The Promises made to the ancestors

A time when the community needs redemption (Occupation)

A time when the community has been scattered (Exile)

The Role of the Environment

Messages and Messengers

The lectionary texts are fully confessional here, as they call out the community as sinful and broken, in need of purification and repentance. Only then will they be equal to the task of returning to the cities promised to their ancestors by God. The Bible usually thought that enemies could only triumph if somehow the protection of the Lord's covenant had been allowed to lapse—through sin, defection to other religions, and mistreatment of the weak (widows, orphans, poor) by the strong (elite landlords, bureaucrats, politicians and military). The way to calculate the severity of the lapse was in measuring the treatment of the poor—who were **not** sent into exile with the Elites, who were, after all, the guilty ones who had caused the people to sin. The Exile, then, was 'proof positive' that the leadership of the people *must* have sinned very badly indeed to merit such a terrible, violent outcome. But the writers of the postexilic period go to some trouble to point out that Deuteronomy is not always the paradigm that should be applied to human suffering: Job is perfectly innocent, according to God, and he suffers anyway, as a 'test case'.

The Bible has traditionally had great trouble mixing monotheism with omnipotence, in assigning blame or reasons for human suffering. If God is all powerful, then God must be 'behind' the train of evil happenings somehow. But perhaps there are other factors which come between God's will and human response: in modern terms, we might talk about random or secondary causation, or perhaps move into an ecological explanation of the interconnectedness of all things. For many parishioners undergoing the time of trial, their very natural question becomes, 'How could a Good God let this happen?' The Bible has often chosen to answer this question with what wisdom scholar James Crenshaw (*Whirlpool of Torment*) has named 'anthropodicy': explaining God's bad behavior (in light of covenant duties to protect the people from enemies) as a result of human bad behavior. This kind of antropodicy is familiar from the testimonies of many survivors of violence: the perpetrator hits us because we caused it, and violence is done and accepted because God 'loves' us.[1] In the end, we are expected to embrace divine violence because it 'restores' the covenant relationship, somehow.

When we apply such concepts to events like the Holocaust, the terrorist attacks of 9/11, or Hurricane Katrina we come to the crux of modern worries about God, power, and punishment. Could anything the Jews had done *really* merit the murder of 6 million Jews? Why didn't God perform His covenant duties to protect the people of the covenant? (It is for this reason that God was put on trial by rabbis interned in Nazi death camps—and found guilty of violating the covenant.) Is it true that things like birth control or supporting the open inclusion of homosexuals as person with rights in our communities *truly* provoke God's punishment of so many innocents, along with suffering nature (which did nothing wrong)? For many scholars who believe in the goodness of God, these traditional answers to suffering are unacceptable and insulting to the very concept of a Redeeming God. They reek of 'state theologians' crafting a 'theology of Empire', attempting to justify the unjust status quo of their own making in order to blame God and counsel acceptance while keeping their own sources of social power in tact.

Like Job, the story of Jesus throws another question mark into this habitual response of blaming the Victim (who must be guilty or they would not be suffering): We are clear that Jesus is Perfectly Innocent, and **this** is the 'Mercy' the Lord 'promised to our ancestors' (Luke 1:72). We now have another way to think about God in the world in relation to suffering: God in Christ has become our co-sufferer, non-violent to the end, and through him, we have a new way of being when we are confronted with violence and despair. Adherence to and emulation of Jesus' behavior ('What would Jesus do?') releases a power, so say believers, that some have named the Holy Spirit. Peace, mutual respect and cooperation begin to invade the human context as the

[1] Depending on your congregation's familiarity and readiness to embrace gender justice, you may choose to supply the masculine language of violence that has been neutered here. There is no example in the Bible of a mother hitting a child or a spouse, though she does act in defense of her husband against his opponent in a fight (with dreadful results all around! Deut 25:11-12).

individual's focus becomes less narrow, more inclusive. Great and strange things are possible in the presence of such a power!

We can now say confidently that God **does** keep those promises of presence, blessing and deliverance, because we have a clear demonstration of a God-in-solidarity-with-us in the Suffering and Redemption of Christ. (Any time we suffer at the hands of evil without ourselves becoming that evil, we may consider ourselves as having been delivered.) Now we look **not** for a battle god who will rape another city in revenge, but to a Servant who calls us friends, and shares our sorrows: the crooked will be made straight, the rough smooth, and all flesh (all mortal creatures, not just humans) shall share in witnessing this salvation from the tired, fragmenting theologies of the empires who tried—but failed—to crush the hearts of Jews and Christians.

All of this changes the shame of being 'lesser' into the joy of redemption! God becomes the source of strength and might, and not the accidents of one's birth or social success. One must 'work' for salvation (drawing water from a well is hard work and one usually performed by women, as are most menial tasks), but bringing it up from inside the earth is a cause for great celebration.

John the Baptist is finally introduced to us, with the ringing words of the prophet Isaiah of Babylon (Isa. 40), the Voice that heralded the coming of Cyrus the Persian who ended the captivity of the Jews in Mesopotamia. No longer were the people a nation, but now they emerged as a religion. No longer Judah, they became the occupied province Yehud, under home rule of the Persian satrapies. They lost the full ability to hold their land, but now had a Torah in their hands with which to face an uncertain, and less glorious future.

Pastoral Prayer for Advent Sunday Two

Lord God,

You have gathered us from east and west,

You have changed our garments

From sorrow to joy,

You have smoothed our path

That we might find You,

And You find us,

Calling our name,

'Righteous Peace,

Godly Glory,'
In a time of promises fulfilled.

All around us, messages arrive,
And prophets unveil Your word:
    On that day, they tell us,
    Fresh waters will cease from the rivers
    And polar bears disappear from the ice floes,
    For the snow will have perished,
    And the ice cap melted,
    All for our hardness of heart!

Yet, as You have promised, so you fulfill:
The time for the Savior has come!
You are Lord of the Message
And God of the Messenger;
Though You have tried us like silver,
You rescue us now from the fire!
You take us from a wilderness
Into a city on high,
With rejoicing in our steps and joy on our lips
As we turn to you in hope.
Mercy and righteousness we crave;
To find them in ourselves
And bear them back to You
In service to the aching world.

Come, Holy Savior, come!

And let the people say,
'Amen!'

Memorable Quotes from our Theological Library

From Catherine Keller, *God and Power: Counter-Apocalyptic Journeys*, a reflection on Revelation, Apocalypse, 9/11, Empire and War:

(On why and how we must NOT turn into our enemies in continuing their hateful behavior, no matter how much we may wish for the revenge of the 'shamed' or triumph of the 'purified'):

> '…*justice* means *acting in consciousness of the relationships that bind us together, relations of a fragile, global interdependence*….The responsible answer to chaos, however, is not dominance but wisdom. Uncertainty will not go away. But our fear of the others with whom we are globally interdependent could dissipate.' (p. 15)

(On the Christian love which acknowledges its roots in Empire and its drive to name all enemies cosmically evil in an imperial apocalypse:)

> '…As the majority of the human and indeed nonhuman population of the planet suffer an undisguised, unjustifiable, delegitimated injustice, we will see not only apocalyptic panic but also movements of self-organizing social justice. We won't get gospel love without justice—only a privatizing, clinging, greedy emotion that yields to fear rather than casts it out. And we won't get apocalyptic justice without love, but only the police state of judgment….In answer, it is not a harmless churchy balance of love and justice that we need, but an *ekklesia* (community) of just love, an eros that readies us for deadly dangers and for delightful surprises.' (pp. 110-111)

Suggestions for Bible Study of Advent C Sunday Two

For this week, we will continue to build on the ideas from last week: Covenant, messages, Exile, Christian behavior, the participation of the natural world in the human-divine dramas of redemption.

Parallel Texts to Use

Psalm 137

Amos

1. Read Psalm 137 aloud together. Use the book of Amos to outline the kinds of 'sins' that brought on the Exile, according to this prophet. When you think of Exile, what comes to your mind? What would be some concerns in bringing a family on foot from Babylon to Jerusalem—and back again? Are you surprised some Jewish communities did not wish to join the great return? It is clear that the Jews blame their enemies as much as they blame themselves for their sorry lot: how can you tell if they have 'moved on' to a new way of thinking about their neighboring states?

What kinds of exiles do modern believers face? (Examples here: people who don't want to leave their homes during hurricanes, wild fires, other disasters; exile from the former view of 'housing' as a form of savings; exile from being the Great American Empire of the 21st century; exile from the status quo of race or gender privilege automatically being the way things are organized, etc.) Who gets 'blamed' as the cause for these various exiles?

Are we going 'into Exile' today? What kind of Exile (from where or what to what or where) are *you* expecting? Fearing? Do you spend much anxious time over thoughts of an upcoming Exile? What do our passages for this week suggest we try to do as we wait for redemption? (Work on self improvement, global justice, keep the law, wait hopefully, expect to see 'signs' in nature, and share the joy of your faith with others of like mind—ie., group solidarity and mutual assistance in times of stress.)

How have the recent economic developments changed or affected your thinking about contemporary 'Exile'? Have some groups been in exile and are now' coming home? How might this change affect those who have NOT been in Exile, but rather those of the previous ruling elite?

2. Why do you think New Testament writers placed so much emphasis on the life of Jesus and his deeds as a fulfillment of prophetic promises made in the Hebrew Bible? Should we expect modern prophets to be as 'weird' as John the Baptist or Ezekiel? (Does that mean we should be paying more attention to comedians like Lewis Black (*Me of Little Faith*) or Sasha Baron Cohen (*Borat, Bruno*)?

What attitudes do the earliest Christians have about the Jews? Do they trash the Covenant or see themselves as the inheritors of it? Where and how does Jesus talk about the Covenant ("Law of Moses", Torah; cf. Matt 5:17; 7:12, 22, 36-40; Luke 16:16, 24:44; John 1:45). Are any of these attitudes the same ones that we hold today? Is it fair to be a 'New Israel' if there is still an old one, which does not wish to be replaced? What should be our relationship to those who are of the Older Covenant? How about those in a covenant that historically came after the 'New' Testament (e.g., Islam)?

3. What kinds of behaviors should characterize the believer? Are they different in adversity compared to good times? Where does the intellect figure in trying to lead a Christian life? Is it more important to **believe** the 'right' things or to **do** the 'right' things? Stephen Covey (*First Things First*) states that we often place the ladders of our lives against the wrong walls; hence, our frustrations and sense of futility. What conclusions do you draw from Matt 25's scene of the Last Judgment? What conclusions might you draw about the religious conflicts in diverse, multicultural societies? Is there a way to balance relative cultural claims against 'universal' truth, without denying the rights of anyone? (Example: if we want to take the Bible seriously as a source for law, are we obligated to kill witches, as some Christian groups in Africa do?) Another example of these tensions might be found in the struggle by the Founding Fathers in their determination of the proper role of religion would play in a new nation: all believed that religion was vital to a democracy, but NOT with 'one' being dominant over others (Steven Waldman, *Founding Faith).*

Suggestions for Church Decorations: High to Low; Trimming the Cosmic Tree

Once again, providing a role for the congregation in making the church ready to receive its Messiah is a way to enhance ownership of the this church season, and presents a way to underscore the issues raised in the readings, sermons, and bible studies.

One of the biggest themes in this Sunday is the notion that God will 'even out' the environment so that everyone will have a commensurate experience, and 'return' from Exile will become easy and available to all. The young and old will not need to climb hills and mountains: they will be lowered. Those in the low places will not flood or have to climb up and out over rocks or sandy dunes: God will raise up the low places. So, we have an image of the natural world being 'leveled' on behalf of disadvantaged humans. There are wonderful implications here for environmental and social practices (one could consider 'society' or 'culture' to be part of humanity's 'natural world'). Clearly, a society where some are at risk from disastrous floods while others suffer from famine needs to find some 'level' place where each group is given the appropriate adjustment of their circumstance. The lame and the outcast (and the young, and those with young, born or not) are a special 'interest' group of the Redeeming God, and every opportunity to ease their way is used.

Hence, decorations for this Sunday might fruitfully play off contrasts of 'high' and 'low': using chairs and stools at the front of the sanctuary, begin with all the adults standing and all the children sitting. As the high-low texts are read, let the little ones stand on their chair (with adult help), and let the adults sit down, so we get a more equal line of heights. This could also be done with a role of paper, or ribbons, or wind socks: the point is that the 'high' parts of the line should become 'lower', and the 'lower' parts should become taller.

If you have someone in your congregation who is in a wheelchair, make them part of this demonstration, setting them two tall adults, who, when seated, will become the same height as the wheelchair (this may not seem very dramatic to the adults, but DO NOT be surprised if the wheel-person weeps in joy at finally being the same as everyone else). If you have a nursing mother, let her and the child in arms start out seated, between two tall adults, and when the children stand on their chairs (with adult help!), let the mother and child stand and be the same height as the children and the seated adults.

If you choose not to use humans as your high/low anchor points, then string a clothesline across the sanctuary, draping it over high items (podium, altar, cross, candlestick, choir) and using a clothes pin, put up on cardstock pictures of valleys that the children have created. When the Scripture is read, let all the liturgists and choir members 'release' all the high points by taking the clothesline off of them, while children pull off the clothespins and valley pictures to 'raise' them up to the level of the 'lowered' high places.

Another option for decorations is to have the Church School create a Tree of Life drawing, super size, mount in on foam core or a sturdy piece of large cardboard (or whatever), and have the children bring it during the offertory and place it against one of the sides of the sanctuary. Next week (after a little strategizing), either have the congregation bring a favorite Christmas tree ornament from home to place on the Cosmic Tree (twisty-ties will anchor the ornament safely to a metal brad or push pin shoved into the tree and its back). If you are uncertain that your tree assembly will support real ornaments, plan for the children to make paper ornaments in Church School. Then, have each family mark their last name on the ornament with a bright crayon, and place it on the tree with double sided tape in lieu of the children's sermon.

Suggestions for Weekly Hymn Selections

Once more, these should not override traditional practices of your congregation, but we provide these here for some suggestions on variations for this Sunday's song selections.

SUNDAY TWO

Pilgrim Hymnal

#104 Comfort, Comfort Ye My People

#110 O Come, O Come Emmanuel

New Century Hymnal

43 Love Divine All Loves Excelling

#110 Now Bless the God of Israel

#115 The Baptist Shouts on Jordan's Shore

#116 O Come, O Come, Emmanuel

#108 Isaiah the Prophet has Written of Old

#120 There's a Voice in the Wilderness

#121 Toda La Tierra (All Earth is Waiting)

Methodist Hymnal

#209 Blessed Be the God of Israel

#210 Toda La Tierra (All the Earth is Waiting)

#211 O Come, O Come Emmanuel

Contemporary

Make Way

Paul Wilbur, The Fire of Your Love

Jami Smith, Salt & Light

John Lennon, Give Peace a Chance

Advent Year C:

Sunday Three

Guide for Pastors, Bible Study Leaders and Others

Introduction

Advent Themes for Year C

The Message or the Messenger?

The Covenant 'In Which You Delight'

Radical Reversals: All in God's Own Good Time

Shame Games and Guilt Quilts: How do we let go?

Day of the Lord, Day of Redemption?

From Exile to Homecoming: How about it?

Sunday Three: Radical Reversals: from Shame to Rejoicing

Readings

Zeph 3:14-20

Psalm = Isaiah 12:2-6

Phil 4:4-7

Luke 3:7-18

Key Theological Concepts:

Judgments: the result of the people having broken the covenant, which results in Exile

Mother-Cities: see Advent Sunday Two, above.

The Divine Warrior: Like most ancient Near Eastern gods, the Holy One of Israel is equipped with a full warrior-god portfolio. Usually, the people expect that this warrior will fight on their behalf, but the prophets often used a surprise interpretation: what happens when the Divine Warrior attacks his own people? This is a very common image in the Book of Job, where God seems to be attacking Job for no reason. If one's Divine Warrior lost the cosmic battle with another warrior god, it meant that his or her people would be conquered. Israel takes a different view: it is not that God was lesser in power than some other god, but rather that God decided to 'hold back' from protection mandated in the Covenant in order to teach the people a lesson about the results of breaking the Covenant.

Day of the Lord: though not mentioned explicitly, this was the time when the people expected the Divine Warrior to appear to fight the national enemies of the king. All wrongs would be righted, all captives returned, and nature, who always fights on the God's side ('the hosts of heaven' are the heavenly bodies that line up and fight on Israel's side at God's command), shares in both the battles and the redemptions foretold.

Shame: both exiles and anyone considered less than 'whole' (the lame, outcast, barren women, menstruating women, etc.) are thought to bear 'shame' because of their condition (shame is a lessening of public status, also endorsed by the one who is shamed). It was a matter of shame that Israel had trusted in God and then been delivered to their enemies. Shame also relates to the metaphor of Sacred Marriage, Israelite style, where the 'female' people 'cheats' on her Divine Husband, causing him shame. When the erring metaphorical wife is exposed to her enemies in punishment for cheating, her public humiliation causes her shame, while it restores the honor of the husband.

Sing and shout: when one is delivered by God, a very public declaration is expected on behalf of the one saved. It is a duty to rejoice and sing praises publically, so that God's faithfulness is underlined and highlighted for other sufferers in the community. Sometimes this turns into a specific kind of Song, a Psalm of Thanksgiving (see Jonah 2:1-9).

Rejoice! and the Peace of God: This is a concomitant sentiment for those who have been redeemed, and so is especially appropriate as a Christian behavior. Rejoicing is a particular sign of the presence of the peace of God, even in times of trial, when the believer is told to pray in a spirit of thanksgiving.

Presence: if God is present in the city or community, then (in theory) protection is in full force and nothing bad will happen.

The Ethics of the Tree: again, we see the images of trees that do not produce good fruit as a metaphor for a society gone awry. Jesus is the Great Gardener who will take out the undesirable plants and replace them with ones that bear good fruit. He winnows, he clears the threshing floor of all the chaff, and gathers the good harvest to him into safety.

Potential Sermon Topics

As before, this Sunday's readings recapitulate topics we have already taken up above: Covenant, Exile, the role of the Natural World, the coming of the Messenger, and the Message of community brokenness which can be made whole. Potential topics that advance or nuance these ideas may be drawn from the theological concepts:

The Divine Warrior (cf. Judges 5):

Blaming the Victims

'Water from the Wells of Salvation'

The Weirdness of the Messenger

Joy in the Face of Despair

Jesus' Ethic of Social Justice

Readings for Sunday Three give us another chance to revisit our continuing themes, as outlined in the theological concepts of Sundays One and Two. Likewise, we have a chance here to enlarge our theological vision of ways that God and Christ are imaged. We can do this by picking up and drawing attention to the clear differences between the Divine Warrior tradition, and the

Grieving City-Mother tradition (which is so beautifully transferred to Jesus in Matt. 23:37, "Jerusalem, Jerusalem, the city that kills the prophets and stones those who are sent to it! How often have I desired to gather your children together as a hen gathers her brood under her wings, and you were not willing!")

Exiles from Judah to Babylon has suffered much shame, both in their humiliating treatment and living conditions as slaves of the empire, but also in the clear results of their grandiose claims: Jerusalem *did* fall, and God *did* permit the elites (who consider themselves the only ones who really count, and are certainly the group responsible for our Bible and its theologies) to be taken prisoner and sent into Exile. This was considered public disproof of the pretentious theologies of conquest under the Deuteronomic reforms of the 7th century, which saw kings of Judah hoping to retake the northern kingdom of Israel, now an Assyrian province, in a surge of national pride. Now the religious officials were left with Royal Psalms that no longer applied, conquest narratives that could only be bittersweet, broken covenants, and a handful of traditions, some written down, some oral, out of which to craft a renewed people.

However much the people may have suffered in Exile, God's promises of a safe (if not splendid) return to the land of Judah, newly called Yehud, with resources to rebuild the Temple in Jerusalem was considered to be a new Exodus and a real redemption from previous sorrows. If the Exile was just punishment for a 'wife'-people who had betrayed her Divine Husband, then the return to Yehud ushered in a new honeymoon, a time of restored intimacy and building trust. During this time, the written and oral traditions begin to come together in a cohesive manner, and now take on the organizational principles of Promise and Fulfillment. God's care had been validated in the national fortunes of the Returnees, and they publically rejoiced in this fact. The euphoria of the Return is the substance of the Psalms of Thanksgiving sung in Zephaniah and Isaiah. New Testament authors feel the same way: they too await hopefully the restoration of their Messiah after his execution, and they counsel this otherworldly hopefulness to all their followers. A new planting and new harvest await patient Christians, no matter how dire the situation may look to outsiders. Public joy is the outcome of this point of view that the reign of God really and truly is 'among us' right now, with drastic implications!

How often do we personally and communally foreclose on hopeful joys by our selective focus on the shames and guilt of the past? Do we have a sense of a real future, or do we merely give lip service to the prospects of living a more meaningful, wholesome life? Indeed, all around are signs of despair that counsel indulgence now in the face of scarcity in the future—but is that a biblically informed response to dreaded change? The coming of the Messiah means that false visions and worldly successes no longer have to be the measuring stick of the community: by recalling God's actions in the past, we can await a better future with genuine hope. The Holy Spirit completes the image of the winds and fire that will sweep through our cynical assumptions. This is Good News!

This Sunday gives us a clear vision of the messenger, John the Baptist, and the fact that sometimes the messenger can be confused with the message (Jesus, in the New Testament's thinking is the 'Word', that is, God's ultimate message to us!). The visual image of the sandal-bearer, long known from ancient Egypt, is the pattern of relationship that John offers to understand his relationship to Jesus. Since few other than the elites actually had shoes in ancient times, the possession of shoes is a tremendous sign of power, chosenness, and divine favor; the earliest Pharaoh (Narmer, of the Early Dynastic Period) is shown simultaneously smiting his enemies, while his much-smaller sandal-bearer follows along behind. John's message is clear: he is not even worthy to be a sandal-bearer (low status servant to the high status leader), much less to be confused with the Messiah!

No matter John's personal quirks in embodying radical repentance —both his food and clothing imply that he 'lives off the land' as the poor do, the message is not compromised. How simple is the Message of Messiah Ethics: it is no more and no less than the Golden Rule of the Jews (the rabbinic form is "What is hateful to you, do not do to another") made flesh with real examples from the world of Roman occupation and unevenly distributed wealth. It applies not only to the 'good' and pious, but to tax collectors and soldiers, too!! All are responsible for the treatment of the poor, even when trapped in a situation where one might easily exploit those with less status. Another Mercy!

Memorable Quotes from the Theological Library:

From James M. Robinson, *Jesus: According to the Earliest Witness*

p. 127-8: '...the kingdom is not something that will take place somewhere, sometime, but is a reality in the present experience of people in the world today....It was in the very real, everyday world that God reigning is very good news. For it was countercultural, and hence gave hope to the hopeless'.

p. 129: 'What made one as carefree as the ravens and lilies was trust in the kingdom of God, God reigning, as a caring Father."

Pastoral Prayer for Advent C Sunday Three

Ancient God, Giver of Life,
You come to us with words of gladness
And bid us rejoice in our restoration.
Though we have known Exile,
We have also experienced Return;
Though we have known shame,
Now we will be subjects of praise!
We ask You, O Lord of All,
Teach us how to rejoice,
Drawing our water from the wells of salvation;
Make us like the good tree that bears fruit,
And the great harvest that feeds all peoples.
Baptize us with wind and fire, passion and love,
That we may welcome You fully into our midst.

And let the people say,
"Amen!"

Suggestions for Bible Study for Advent C Sunday Three

Experiencing the pain of the Exile will cast the joy of the Good News into sharp relief. We can revisit a few earlier texts here, as well as some 'classics' on suffering:

Book of Amos

Book of Lamentations

Psalm 79, 88, 137

Study questions:

1. There was a clear difference between the elite leaders' view of the Day of the Lord and the view of the prophets (cf., Amos and Hosea, Jeremiah, etc.). What accounts for that? How could the leaders have gotten it so very wrong? How did theology collude to create the expectation that God would support the people, no matter what, simply on grounds of nationalism?
   Do you see evidence of a 'Day of the Lord' theology in the modern world? What happens when that day is 'dark, and not light'? What does Day of the Lord theology do to advance global harmony and justice? How does it hinder it? (Are you worried about that?)

2. Simply sit with the Book of Lamentations, taking turns reading it aloud, and experience it. Traditionally said to have been composed by Jeremiah at the time of the fall of Jerusalem in 586 BCE to the Babylonians, it is composed in the form of a funeral lament that sounds very eerie in Hebrew. How is Jerusalem described (human images, natural images, abstract images)? What are the particular elements that the Lamentations authors seem to find so very devastating? Would these elements have the same impact now? (How many TV 'reality shows' are predicated upon the artificial introduction of some of these elements into 'normal' people's experiences?) How does a faithful person cope with this sort of pain? (hint: the lament Psalm, whether personal (Psalm 88) or national (Psalm 79) is a traditional biblical response which presumes God is really there and really cares!)

3. Who in public life can you think of who embodies the prophetic role? Are they also like John or Ezekiel—weird, dramatic, and erratic? Are their ethics the same as the Messiah's? If not, to what 'authority' do they appeal for 'back-up'? Why aren't there more prophets coming out of religious settings with Messiah ethics? (a good reformer like Ralph Nader or Al Gore, or a comedian like Jon Stewart, Stephen Colbert or Lewis Black can be used to highlight the diffusion of the public role of prophet into secular spheres) Has anyone in your personal life held the role of prophet for you? Why? How did it work out? Do we hear the cry of the prophets today? Who does our culture want us to listen to?

Suggestions for Church Decorations

Rejoice always: Have the children make a variety of signs in a host of colors which proclaim 'Rejoice' and 'Rejoice always'. Place them on a clothesline or your Cosmic Tree hung with ornaments.

Coat Exchange: Have the children decorate a huge cardboard box or garbage can, with festive wrapping papers. Encourage the congregation to fill it with their second coat. Leave it in the sanctuary and ritually deliver it to some needy group on Christmas Eve.

Winnowing: decorate the sanctuary with rakes and pitchforks. Have the children make little signs (6"x 10" or so), some reading 'mercy' and others reading 'greed'. Put the 'mercies' in front of the fork; put the 'greeds' behind. At the time of the offertory, have the children gather all the 'mercies' and put them in an offering basket for the altar.

Suggestions for Weekly Hymn Selections

SUNDAY THREE

Pilgrim Hymnal

#111 Of the Father's Love Begotten

#114 Lift Up Your Heads, Ye Mighty Gates

#131 Lo, How a Rose E'er Blooming

New Century Hymnal

#102 Oh How Shall I Receive You

#109 With Joy Draw Water

#114 Return, My People

#117 Lift Up Your Heads, Ye Mighty Gates

#118 Of the Parent's Heart Begotten

Methodist Hymnal

#184 Of the Father's Love Begotten

#213 Lift Up Your Heads, Ye Mighty Gates

Contemporary

Hillsong, God is Good

Andre Crouch, Soon, Very Soon

Bible Ringtones, Sing Alleluia to the Lord

Safety Harbor, The Canticle of the Turning

Advent Year C:

Sunday Four

Guide for Pastors, Bible Study Leaders and Others

Introduction

Advent Themes:

The Message or the Messenger?

Radical Reversals: All in God's Own Good Time

The Covenant 'In Which You Delight'

Shame Games and Guilt Quilts: How do we let go?

Day of the Lord, Day of Redemption?

From Exile to Homecoming: How about it?

Sunday Four: 'She Who Believed' and Radical Reversals

Readings:

Micah 5:2-5

Psalm 80:1-7

Hebrews 10:5-10

Luke 1:46-55

'Shepherd of Israel': ultimately, this is God who shepherds the people (Psalm 23), and the iconographic king, David, whose biography places him in Bethlehem as a shepherd. Additionally, in the ancient Near East, city kings were often imaged as shepherds who fed the 'flocks' of the city-mother/goddess. Jesus as 'Good Shepherd' is drawn from this pool of imagery.

'Shame, guilt, and punishment': Israel and Judah's guilt caused God's punishment for breaking the covenant (a failure to do justice), which in turn becomes a great source of shame and suffering.

'Human emotions': all these (anger, face shining with pleasure) embodied expressions are considered applicable to God. The hope of prayer is to 'move' God from having an 'angry countenance' (lit., 'hot nose') to face smoothed of frustration and wreathed in smiles.

'Divine Warrior: however various troubles may have come about, the expectation is that God will come when called, and right national and personal wrongs.

'Failure of the sacrificial cult': while the New Testament takes the view that the cult is no longer necessary because of the sacrifice of Jesus (however understood), this idea has already been anticipated by the prophets and the psalms (cf. Psalm 50)

'High/Low in the Human Landscape': just as we saw the Redeemer God level the playing field environmentally to assist the Exiles' safe return to their land, Mary's Song plays off the Song of Hannah in 1 Samuel, and depicts the same saving actions, now leveling human society and status.

Potential Sermon Topics

We have finally arrived at some very classic texts for the Advent season: it is most natural to assume that the Song of the Madonna will take pride of place in this Sunday's theological message. The passage from the Judean editor of Micah places the Shepherd of Israel tradition in the little town of Bethlehem (literally, 'house of Bread'—now the living Bread that will feed the weary world), and Psalm 80 underscored that the people have suffered as they wait for the deliverance and continued love promised by the Davidic covenant. This is the covenant that could not be broken, but could be transformed out of all recognition by the circumstances of foreign occupation of Yehud (Persian conquest of Judah) and Palastina (Roman conquest of Judah). As always, suffering causes shame, as onlookers blame the victims and make them objects of scorn and derision.

As we come to the actual arrival of the Messiah in the most non-threatening way possible—a defenseless infant!—we meet a theme we have not seen previously, but which will be fully developed throughout the rest of the church year. This is the 'replacement' of the failed sacrificial cults of the state kings in Jerusalem with the Christian vision of a world where physical sacrifice is no longer necessary or even effective.

Often when a country attempts to revive national sentiments and inspire confidence, the leadership tries to include all the external trappings of religious observance as a piece of the overall view that the state is in 'good standing' with the universe. However, from the time of the 8th century BCE, when we first start to see the inequality of poverty reflected in both archaeology and text (Micah, Amos, Hosea, and later First Isaiah and Jeremiah), and *this*, according to the prophets, cannot be cancelled out by oceans of sacrificial blood and insincere cultic worship! While the prophets usually cast this defection from the covenant (which tried to guarantee fair resources to all) in terms of the city-goddess-wife who has 'cheated' on her Divine Warrior husband with 'other gods' (that is, top-down economic and social organization which crushes the poor and the defenseless), the practice their withering scorn takes on and denounces is actually the inequalities of poverty and the sins of personal and national greed. Formal worship, then, is more of a bribe the leaders try to use to diffuse God's anger at the real state of affairs. God's penchant for the dramatic reversal of fortune is an outcome of this frustration and anger at the balance of formal religion versus true civic virtue. The Divine Warrior gleefully changes things around in a radical way—clearing the game board and starting over with newly leveled conditions!

Mary's Magnificat picks up on the beloved Song of Hannah, the barren woman of early Israel, who made her case for improved fertility directly to God, and was rewarded with a child who would become kingmaker and covenant arbiter—the prophet Samuel. Of course, barrenness was never an issue for Mary of Nazareth—far from it! Instead, she is embarrassingly fertile, which causes complications because of her betrothed status. The author of Luke is busy getting Mary out of town for the beginning of her pregnancy, which, given social customs, must have been as much a matter for worry and fear as it was for astonished belief and expectancy.

Mary could just as easily be stoned to death for her breach of virginity while betrothed as become the mother of the Savior. No wonder Elizabeth pours out blessings upon her, realizing both the special quality of her unborn child (as her unborn baby, John the Baptist, gets an early jump on announcing the coming of the Messiah with a well placed kick) *and* Mary's own special qualities of faithful trust. "Blessed is she who believed" offers us a new understanding of Mary's role in redemption as more than just a vessel; it suggests that Mary's cooperative faith was a requirement before the whole Incarnation plan could proceed. Some scholars speculate on the negative overtones of the overpowering presence of God, fathering a child on a girl child barely into puberty, but with this verse we may lay those speculations to rest. Mary is not the subject of divine rape as are the mothers of Greek heroes; she is a consenting believer whose very belief solidifies and makes manifest the truly embodied nature of redemption.

Mary's song, then, is an expression of her faith and her knowledge of what the coming of the Messiah will mean for those in the covenant and outside of it. The high will become low; the barren will be fruitful, and the poor will finally eat. The 'Mighty One of Israel', a title developed from covenants renewed by Jacob and his family in Genesis, is finally, fully 'on duty' to deliver and protect. Chesed (mercy; see Sunday One) has won out over anger, action has replaced waiting, and all life awaits the outcome of these unexpected reversals, which are no more than the ongoing results of the covenant relationship between the people and God. Note that no violence is done in the action of these reversals: the wealthy share the state of the poor, not death; the proud are only 'scattered in their thoughts', not scattered as body parts by a vengeful conquering army! Strange days are afoot, and we are all blessed with the excitement of the coming days.

How often have we waited without any real expectation of change, either within ourselves or around us? How many times are we tempted to substitute the formal elements of our faith for a radical reversal that trusts in an ongoing relationship between the people and God every day? Are we actually ready to rejoice and believe? What might it take to get us 'on board' the Good Ship Messiah and sail into a just and sustainable future for all Earth's creatures?

Memorable Quotes from the Theological Library

J. Philip Newell, *Echo of the Soul: The Sacredness of the Human Body*

P. 48 (generally on 'living in' the reign of God that is already here): 'Deep in our souls are the promptings of love's strength. When we use the power of force creatively or defensively in our lives and world we are being called at the same time to release from our depths the even greater strength of love. '

p. 42: 'The capacity for power that has been placed deep within us is given that we too may hold back forces of violence in our world and in our own selves.

P. 40: '…it is important not to define ourselves primarily in terms of our failures and weaknesses. Our neglect and abuse of strength are not the deepest expressions of who we are. In fact they are false expressions of who we are. We are made in the image of God. Woven into the fabric of our souls is a capacity for true strength.

Pastoral Prayer for Advent C Sunday Four

Loving Father God, Womb of the Universe,
You have called greatness out of what was small,
And fed Your flocks with strength and righteousness.
You have turned us from scorn to delight,
From grief to dancing, from dark to light
As we approach this Season of the growing dark.
We are low, but you have brought us high up;
We are mortal, but you have promised us more:
That You do indeed reign every day.
Blessed are we among peoples!
Mercy and might are Your gifts to all,
Promises fulfilled light our way.
Ravens and lilies teach us to trust,
And the Messiah shows us the way.
Holy is Your Name!!

Suggestions for Bible Study of Advent C Sunday Four

This weeks Bible Study texts will examine the theological themes of this Sunday as they appeared in the earlier texts on which they play.

The Song of Hannah (I Sam 2:1-10)

Psalm 1

Psalm 50

Study questions:

5. Hannah's Song uses many different images to characterize the nature and actions of God. Which of these resonates most with your experience? Which do you think become the most prominent in Mary's version of this Song? Are there theological implications in the changes taking place in moving from Samuel to Luke?

6. Notice that Psalm One (usually thought of as a postexilic 'preface' to reading the Psalter) confidently expresses the same tone about God's judgment of the wicked as do the Songs of Hannah and Mary. How does the natural world provide analogies for understanding the different fates for the good and the wicked. Are we so comfortable today with the notion of 'wickedness' as the sole characteristic of certain people or groups? Is the black/white duality of this kind of thinking a hindrance to establishing real Messiah ethics, or does it help us along the way? Is it actually God who is doing the punishing in Hannah's Song or Psalm One?

7. Psalm 50 is pretty astonishing, and a serious trial for those who only know God and Christ as Divine Warriors, always ranged on their particular side of an issue. Those who hope that the excellence of their liturgies, the proper recital of their prayers, and their formal lip service to the duties of the covenant will serve them on the Day of the Lord are wrong. The Book of Revelation does not outweigh the Gospels.

Who might have written this scathing critique of public worship and private piety? The Mighty One is God the Lord—that is a complex statement! It means that the specific Covenant Lord of the ancestors ("God of the Fathers" in Genesis) is ALSO the Creator ('God' or Elohim in Hebrew) AND the Redeeming Divine Warrior ('Lord' or YHWH in Hebrew). How do we make a theology of worship that can stand up to this Triune God's fullness of character? How do we understand the death of Jesus, given the rejection of blood sacrifice in this passage? Which aspects of the divine character are most important to the New Testament authors as they paint their portraits of Jesus? Which are most important to *you?*

Suggestions for Church Decorations

Now is the time to 'pull out all the stops' on your traditional Christmas practices: trees, nativities, church school pageants—all these are appropriate, as is blessing of animals, gifts for the poor, and special dedications of vocation within the Church. Let everyone bring their joy to the altar and offer it as a gift to the Baby Messiah.

Hopefully, enough good ideas will have surfaced about the meaning of High/Low in the previous weeks to allow you to build on that theme with congregational participation. Some ideas: baskets of food that will go to the poor after the service should be placed on the floor. During the offertory, have the congregation start out with their purses and wallets held high; as a high/low text is read and offerings are collected, let them lower their 'signs' of monetary success, and instead lift up the baskets. Each family might prepare their own basket, so that the children are fully involved in 'giving' as a form of worship.

Other forms of high/low exchanges in radical reversal: turn a tv remote held high into a family game board lifted up from the floor; turn a store-bought coffee in a Styrofoam cup into a home coffee-pot; turn a bottle of water into a pitcher that purifies water. Take the baby out of the manger and put a crown on him…you get the idea!

If you live in a cold climate, everyone in the congregation might start out the offertory wearing an extra piece of outerwear or a coat. Let them come forward and take off this 'extra' blessing and place it in a big pile to be distributed to the needy later.

Suggestions for Weekly Hymn Selections

SUNDAY FOUR

Pilgrim Hymnal

#107 Let All Mortal Flesh Keep Silence

#109 Watchman, Tell Us of the Night

New Century Hymnal

#103 Watcher, Tell Us of the Night

#106 My Heart Sings Out with Joyful Praise
#107 Awake! Awake, and Greet the New Morn
#113 Little Bethlehem of Judah
#119 My Soul Gives Glory to My God
#123 Mary, Woman of the Promise
#345 Let All Mortal Flesh Keep Silence

Methodist Hymnal
#198 My Soul Gives Glory to My God
#215 To a Maid Engaged to Joseph
#626 Let All Mortal Flesh

Contemporary
John Starke, I will Rejoice in the Lord
Jonathan David, It is Good
Chris Tomlin, Exalted
Stephen Schwartz, Bless the Lord
Safety Harbor, The Canticle of the Turning

Theologian's PostScript

We have tried to provide with a mixture of resources drawn from two primary repositories of traditions: text and the arts. Worship that is enlivened by arts and congregational participation becomes lively, relevant and transforming. As such, it makes a wonderful setting for textual study that re-encounters the familiar with new appreciation and methods of interpretation.

One theological perspective that we have tried to highlight here is that of the value of the created world, its presence as a positive player in the dramas of Scripture, and its current state of endangerment. This is deliberate, and we encourage you do even more to place these issues, fully endorsed by the UCC as subject matter for congregational study and action, in front of your people. We have also tried to undercut divisive, dualistic readings of Scripture with a renewed emphasis on the model of Jesus in Messiah Ethics derived from ongoing studies of the Sayings Gospel Q. Justice is not optional; it is obligatory, but may be pursued in many different ways by diverse groups within and beyond the congregation.

Our very best wishes for a blessed Advent Season and a resplendent Christmas! May the peace of God in Christ, which passes all understanding, be in your hearts and minds as you go in peace to love and serve the World!

In Peace,

Carole R. Fontaine

Taylor Professor of Biblical Theology and History, Andover Newton Theological School

Theologian-in-Residence, Pass-a-Grille Beach Community Church (UCC), St. Pete Beach, Florida

Andover Newton Theological School

World Book Encyclopedia, Religion Editor

Theologian-in –Residence, Pass-a-Grille Video Academy Program

Rev. Dr. Keith Haemmelmann

Director, Pass-a-Grille Video Academy Program

Pass-a-Grille Community Church, UCC

Pass-a-Grille, Florida

Theological Library:

Suggestions for Further Reading

John Dominic Crossan, God and Empire: Jesus Against Rome, Then and Now
(New York: HarperCollins, 2008).

J. Dominic Crossan, *Who Killed Jesus? Exposing the Roots of Anti-Semitism in the Gospel Story of The Death of Jesus* (New York: HarperCollins, 1996).

Catherine Keller, *God and Power: Counter-Apocalyptic Journeys* (Minneapolis: Fortress, 2005).

J. Philip Newell, *Echo of the Soul: The Sacredness of the Human Body* (Harrisburg, PA: Morehouse Publishing, 2000.)

James M. Robinson, *Jesus: According to the Earliest Witness* (Minneapolis: Fortress, 2007).

www.ingramcontent.com/pod-product-compliance
Ingram Content Group UK Ltd.
Pitfield, Milton Keynes, MK11 3LW, UK
UKHW041834200726
13854UKWH00003BA/1124